Contents

Introduction to eBAY

Grasping the Opportunity

It seemed like an ordinary day when I arrived home after a long morning of teaching: but nothing could be further from the truth. As I unlocked the back door and stepped inside my kitchen I experienced my 'eureka' moment.

The clutter in the kitchen screamed at me! The noise was deafening! For the first time I saw that my kitchen was jam packed with things. It was full to bursting with items, few of which were even remotely connected to the preparation of food.

My kitchen shelves were laden with copious cups and saucers, dozens of dishes, vintage vases and glass items of every size and type. The work surfaces were swamped in ceramics and having run out of horizontal space on which to house my acquisitions I had taken to hanging things on the walls and even suspending them from the ceiling!

Most were 'bargains' too good to resist, though you needed to be a collector to 'get it'. Sadly this jumble was not confined to the kitchen. The plethora of possessions was duplicated throughout the house. Each room was furnished with plunder from my frequent forays to antique fairs and to cross a room was to negotiate an assault course of chairs, tables and book cases. No material was unrepresented and no era excluded.

What could it be like to live with me? It was in this insightful split second that realised I needed to change. I was determined to scale down but the question was how? A chance encounter a couple of weeks later provided the answer.

As a teacher of antiques and collectables my work takes me all over the country and on this occasion I found myself in London. Attending the course were two sisters who were keen to further their knowledge of old china and I found myself sitting with them in the break. As I was dunking a digestive in my tea they casually uttered the words that changed my life.

The sisters (who could barely rustle up a GCSE between them) told me that they knew nothing about computers and even less about ceramics but had both made so much money selling retro china on eBay that they had given up their jobs.

I was dumbfounded. As a collector I was familiar with different ways of buying and selling but had purposely given eBay (and everything requiring an electrical plug) a wide berth. Clearly I was missing a trick: I could not wait to get home and log on.

It took time and tears but I eventually mastered the art of trading on eBay. I got down to the task of selling the offending items. As the clutter thinned my coffers swelled and far from mourning the pieces that I sold I forgot I ever owned them.

I shared my enthusiasm with my students and urged them to look at eBay. But as we talked I became aware of their concerns about using this cutting edge site and I identified a gap in the market for someone to offer hands-on eBay lessons. As a technologically untalented individual who understood the barriers I realised that this someone was me.

I approached the managers at the newly formed eBay UK with the idea of presenting hands-on lessons for mature students. Being internet savvy, they were initially bemused that such tuition was required but soon warmed to the idea.

The first classes caused a media sensation. They were filmed for *Tonight With Trevor MacDonald* and I was invited onto the *Richard & Judy Show*. I was interviewed for Radio 4's *In Business*. At the end of the first course two eBay managers, Garreth Griffiths and Richard Ambrose (pictured), travelled down to meet the students and answer questions. They were charming and informative and came armed with gifts for my students.

eBay is Perfect for the Older Generation

eBay is a sensation. It was originally embraced by collectors who were delighted to partake of the global market. Young people have been quick to latch on to its benefits. However eBay represents a wonderful opportunity for older people.

Why eBay is Ideal for Older People – Buying

- eBay is a one-stop shop where you can buy most things

- Many items are offered at competitive prices

- You can find new and used items on eBay

- eBay offers shops, auctions and Buy-It-Now

- Many sellers offer a returns policy

- eBay is perfect for anyone with mobility issues

- PayPal facilitates safe online payment

- Focused collecting is an absorbing hobby

Rob's Steal!

Rob, 62, has recently retired. At last he has time to devote to music. Rob is a singer songwriter and has set up his own recording studio. He has tracked down specialist equipment and classic rock greats at bargain prices.

Sheila's Meals

Sheila, 84, has recently become an eBay seller. She plans to exchange her house for a chic retirement apartment. She is selling the surplus items and intends to spend money eating out in style.

Why eBay is Ideal for Older People – Selling

- Offload surplus possessions before moving

- Stay put but simplify your life

- Tastes change and some items no longer suit.

- Retired or semi-retired people have time to sell

- eBay trading enhances computer and internet skills

- Make money whilst losing the clutter

- Reinvent your look, home, hobbies on eBay

- Sell items for your family and friends

Cora is Cool

Cora amazed the family! When her teenage granddaughter declared her wedges were too tight Cora nonchalantly offered to list them on her account. Cool or what?

Brief History of eBay

eBay broke the mould. Billions of items have been traded on eBay and it is amazing to consider that it has been around for less than 15 years and began, not with a bang but a whimper.

Pierre Omidyar

It was in 1995 that Pierre Omidyar launched his revolutionary site. He was not a native of California but born in Paris, the only son of French Iranian parents who moved to the USA in 1973.

Move to the USA

Pierre had an aptitude for computers and studied computer science at University. The 1980s saw the dawn of computers and Pierre moved around from job to job. He joined General Magic to work with the internet, the most recent excitement for computer buffs for whom the thrills were about to escalate.

World Wide Web

In 1990 Sir Tim Berners-Lee created the World Wide Web, the means by which the internet gained commercial potential. There instantly grew up enormous excitement surrounding the possibilities, though few knew exactly how to exploit it.

Internet Entrepreneurs £$

The potential seemed limitless and the anticipation mounted. There sprang up a new type of financial speculator called internet entrepreneurs who threw money at even half-credible ideas.

A Productive Weekend

It was during this frantic phase of internet fever that Pierre sat down to write a program. He wanted to create the perfect market to enable collectors to trade together. This simple program which comprised an internet auction was hurriedly knocked out in a single weekend. In a few years it had matured into the legendary site that has rocked the commercial world.

Launched in 1999 there are now 14 million regular British users

Hundreds Versus Millions

Roadside Sale – potential market = hundreds
eBay.co.uk potential market = millions & millions

eBay's Wider Role

Computer and Internet Skills

Master eBay and you will progress a range of skills including word processing and digital photography. Denman College, the Woman's Institute Headquarters (shown above) offers hands-on courses in eBay trading. Denman welcomes everyone.

Re-cycling

eBay is the ultimate re-cycling vehicle. Collectors from all over the world snap-up the things that would otherwise be discarded and create archives. Future generations will reap the benefits.

Employment

Over 178,000 people in this country make their living or part of it selling on eBay. You can use eBay to bolster a low income.

Ethical trading

Every effort is taken to keep the site moral and ethical. The items that are banned are those that might compromise the high standards set by eBay. Members are encouraged to police the site and report questionable auctions.

Charity

Charitable donations are an integral and high profile part of eBay which raises huge sums for a variety of causes.

eBay Overview

Basic Facts of eBay

- eBay brings together buyers and sellers

- eBay do not usually become involved in the transaction

- Buyers pay the sellers direct

- Items are sent from the seller to the buyer

- Items offered on eBay are not vetted

- All traders must be over 18 years old

- You have to register to trade on eBay

- It is free to buy but sellers are charged a small fee

- eBay is a community where members police the site

- PayPal is eBay's preferred payment system

- PayPal is free to buyers but sellers pay a fee

- eBay is available 24 hours a day, 7 days a week

What Can You Buy?

eBay has a stunning choice of clothes for mature people. You can find a bargain outfit for that special occasion from the comfort of your own home and free parking! The following day you can put it up for auction!

Home-making thrives on eBay. Buy curtains, furnishings and bedding, new or used, auction or Buy-it-Now.

Everyday health and beauty items can be found on eBay. Many motivated sellers offer postal discount on multiple purchases.

Toys, games and puzzles are found in abundance on eBay. You can buy cutting edge video games or root out the special things that you cherished as a child.

Courses, breaks, holidays and tickets are all on eBay. With prudence you will pay a fraction of the regular price but you have to proceed cautiously, do your research and scrutinise the seller.

What Sells Best

Named, marked and branded items sell better than unidentified ones. It is difficult to assess quality from pictures so buyers favour things they know. Anonymity is not a plus on eBay.

Cannot name the maker or designer? Try an era. Your item will benefit from coming from a particular era. Victorian, Art Deco, Fifties, Sixties.

Items from well known sets and particularly ceramic and glass collectables. They get damaged and need replacing.

Collectable pieces and particularly those that were made in this country but for which there is a global market. There is worldwide demand for Dr Who memorabilia, Clarice Cliff china and Festival of Britain items.

There is a strong demand for antique furniture and particularly chic, timeless, utilitarian items such as this fine leather chair.

Understanding eBay Buying

- Find an item

- Study the information about the item

- Take note of the condition

- Carefully view the pictures

- Note the cost of shipping

- Check you can comply with method of payment

- Check the credibility of the seller

- Check the seller's feedback and read comments

- Contact the seller via link with questions

- Place a bid

- Watch the auction progress in My eBay

- If outbid – bid again or look elsewhere

- On winning the item use link in My eBay to pay

- Check item when it arrives

- All well? Leave positive feedback

- Receive positive feedback from seller

www.getitmoved.co.uk

Buying on eBay is not restricted to items that can be sent in the post. Try the dedicated eBay transport company shown above.

Understanding eBay Selling

- The seller puts an item up for auction

- The seller uses pictures to attract the buyers

- The seller lists the item in an appropriate category

- The seller uses key words in the auction title

- The seller describes the item including flaws

- The seller decides the length of the auction (1 to 10 days)

- The seller chooses the start price

- The seller states the cost of shipping

- The seller can select to use a reserve price (£50+)

- Seller watches auction and answers questions

- The winner receives an email from eBay

- The seller sends an online invoice

- Or the buyer pays (includes P & P) via the links

- The seller carefully packs and sends the item

- Both buyer and seller leave positive feedback

Research shows that the average household is sitting on £452 worth of unwanted items. For the over 50s this sum is probably higher!

Mean Maud's Miserly Methods

Maud sniffs out bargains by selecting auctions that are ending soon and scours through for those with no bids.

Maud makes her bids non-round sums - so, not £8 but £8.04 as it gives her the edge over like-minded buyers.

Maud pays for her bargains with PayPal as it is free for buyers, has inbuilt safeguards and saves the cost of a stamp.

Maud does her Christmas shopping on eBay in the summer as there are fewer rival bidders in August than in December.

Maud seeks out sellers who offer a returns policy so she is not stuck with anything she does not like!

Maud buys DVD's on eBay so that she can watch them at her leisure before selling them.

Maud buys and sells clothes on eBay and for special occasions she selects new items only.

Maud keeps an eye out in charity shops for interesting items to sell on eBay.

Maud made a bulk purchase of ten Midwinter cups and saucers though she only required four. She sold the remaining six individually. Her quartet of cups came for free!

Maud never needs to utter that offensive phrase 'have you kept the receipt?'

Tour of the Site

Finding the Site

Type www.ebay.co.uk into your browser and press enter.

This brings up eBay UK's home page. Take a good look at this page as this gives a taste of all that eBay has to offer.

First Time on the Home Page

Your first visit to eBay will bring up a special version of the home page that offers guidance to newcomers. From then on you reach the regular homepage, part of which is shown below:

Home Page

You should think of the home page as the reception area of a large corporation with several 'doors' (known as links) that take you to other parts of the site. These links give an indication of what you will find when you select them.

At first glance the home page looks busy and daunting but, from the point of view of getting started, there are only a few areas that need concern you. These are:

- Registration Link

- Categories

- eBay Search Engine

- Homepage Links

eBay's home page is also its shop window and offers news of offers and short cuts to exciting links.

Registration Link

You can browse on eBay for as long as you need to familiarise yourself with the site, but to trade you have to register. You can do this by clicking onto the link on the home page.

You do not have to register to browse on eBay. Take time to investigate the site and familiarise yourself with the pages. Return to the home page if you lose your way.

Categories

The categories are listed on the left-hand side of the home page. They are listed alphabetically commencing with Antiques and finishing with Wholesale and Job Lots and Everything Else.

There are millions of items offered for sale at any one time so these categories are divided into sub-categories and sub-sub categories, making it easy to locate particular items.

eBay Categories

Antiques
Art
Baby
Books, Comics & Magazin
Business, Office & Industri
Cars, Parts & Vehicles
Clothes, Shoes, Accessori
Coins
Collectables
Computing
Consumer Electronics
Crafts
Dolls & Bears

eBay Search Engine

The eBay pages contain many opportunities to use the search engine. The first you will come across is situated at the top of the home page, but they appear throughout the site.

Keyword Search

The search engine is where you type appropriate keywords to find a particular item.

They work by linking the words you select with those in the auction title.

Find | mustard pot

The keyword search for mustard pot reveals a list of 335 auctions in a range of categories including silver, pottery and books. It finds all the auctions with those words in the title.

Main Home Page Links

Buy   Sell   My eBay   Community   Help

Site Map

On the top right-hand side of the home page are the main links. They consist of Buy, Sell, My eBay, Community and Help. Just beneath Help is Site Map.

Site Map

Site Map is particularly useful for novices. It is a complete index of eBay pages and lists everything that you will find on the site.

Home > **Site Map**

Site Map

It is presented in 5 sections:

Buy, Sell, My eBay, Community, Help

Site Map offers a way ahead for every situation that baffles you. Think of the map in London's underground railway – you refer to it when you seek a new direction and would be lost without it.

The example on the right shows the Selling Activities section. This is just a small section of Site Map but illustrates how useful and pragmatic it can be. If you have any concerns about your buying or selling activities you should take a peek at Site Map.

Selling Activities

· Revise Your Item
· Add to Your Item Description
· Change Your Item's Gallery Image
· Manage Bidders
· Cancel Bids on Your Listing
· End Your Listing
· Relist Your Item
· Manage Your Shop
· Manage Your Counters
· Search Want It Now
  See all Selling Activities...

Buy

Buy is the link that brings up the long
list of categories. You should click on
this link when looking to buy an item.

Buy Sell My eBay

Browse Categories

All items ending soon

Shopping Tools

Buying Tips

Buy Safely

eBay Mobile

However this link offers a range of
alternative tools designed to help. Rest
the cursor on Buy to reveal what is on
offer.

When you have grasped the basics
you can explore the Shopping Tools section where you will find
bookmarks and toolbar information.

The Buying Tips are worth investigating. Some time in the
future you might want to link eBay to your mobile phone. The
pain of the learning curve is compensated for by the freedom.

Sell

Sell My eBay

When you are ready to create your auction
you will click on this link to start the
process. Sell an item brings up the online
form which enables you to start the
auction creation process.

Sell an item

How to sell

Sell Safely

Sell for Charity

Business Centre

Powerseller Hub

However this link contains far more and
you just have to rest the cursor on the sell
link to reveal what else it contains.

Some of the links concern professional sellers and the support
provided by eBay. However, there are hints and tips to assist
you to make the most of the selling opportunity.

The emphasis is on safe selling and the measures that you can
take to ensure things go well. In recent years eBay has made it
easy to make charitable donations.

My eBay

This is one of the most useful areas on the site and will be the place where you come to each time that you log on. My eBay is where all your browsing, bidding, buying and selling activities are to be found in one convenient place. A few years ago eBay introduced My Messages which enables you to trade safely. You should ensure that you take full advantage of this. My eBay is explained fully in Chapter 7.

Community

eBay is far more than a trading site. The eBay ethos is that traders look out for each other. Most are courteous and give fellow traders the benefit of the doubt.

What's New

Share your thoughts! Write an eBay Review or Guide.

Say No to Spoofs! Check out the Safety Centre.

More Listings, Less Times. Use a Listing Tool.

eBay managers rely on community members to police the site to keep it legal, moral and safe. The community boards encourage members to chat to each other and respond to each others questions.

When a member posts a question typically they are overwhelmed by offers of help from traders. Members use the chat boards to mull over problems and let off steam. The enormous growth of eBay has not detracted from the spirit of generosity, kindness and co-operation that prevails on eBay.

Help

There will probably come a time when you will need some help. There have been so many transactions undertaken on eBay and so many predicaments resolved that you will not have a query that they have not come across time and time again. There are dedicated Help pages that are bound to find a solution to your problem.

Feedback

Your Online Reputation

Of all the outstanding ideas embraced by eBay, feedback has to be the best. To understand it you should think of how you proceed in your everyday activities. When employing a plumber or solicitor you would probably ask around amongst friends and seek a recommendation. Feedback is the online equivalent of a professional reputation and when used wisely it can help ensure that your transactions go well.

How Feedback Works

On receiving the goods, and providing everyone is happy, the buyer completes a brief affirmative report on the seller. There may be rare occasions when a buyer has a bad experience which needs to be conveyed to the community. The comments, which are collectively referred to as their feedback, are helpful to other eBayers.

Feedback Form

There are three aspects to the feedback form:

1. Rating – Positive, Negative or Neutral
2. Statement – How it went (see p23)
3. Detailed Seller Rating – Completed by buyers only

Feedback Rating – Score

The feedback rating, which is positive, negative or neutral, is expressed as a score and is the difference between the number of members who left a positive rating and the number that left a negative rating. (Positive feedback gains a point, negative loses a point, neutral does not count.) It is slightly different for multiple sales and depends if the sales occurred in different weeks.

(485 ☆)

Feedback Rating – Percentage

What is of great significance to fellow traders is that feedback is also expressed as a percentage. Negative feedback is set against positive feedback and expressed as a percentage.

Best Use of Feedback

When used together, just a glance at the feedback score and percentage are a critical insight into the likely reliability of a trader. However, sometimes negative feedback is left unfairly and you have an opportunity to read the comments and decide about the trader for yourself. Click on See for detailed feedback.

This seller has only achieved 94.1% positive feedback on 225 transactions. You should read the feedback comments before trading with this eBayer.

Check the seller's reputation
Score: 225 | 94.1% Positive
See detailed feedback

No such concerns about this trader's track record of 100% positive on over 19,000 transactions!

Check the seller's reputation
Score: 19575 | 100% Positive
See detailed feedback

Feedback Statement

⊕ Good buyer, prompt payment, valued customer, highly recommended.

⊕ Well packed. Good communication. Pleased with item. Many thanks

The statement is an opportunity to express appreciation and this section undoubtedly increases the goodwill on the site. eBay encourage constructive comments that describe the strengths of a trader.

Detailed Seller Ratings

Buyers are also invited to complete a more detailed and entirely anonymous assessment of the service the seller provided. This includes accuracy, communication, the time it took to arrive.

Item as described	★ ★ ★ ★ ⯪
Communication	★ ★ ★ ★ ⯪
Dispatch time	★ ★ ★ ★ ⯪
Postage and packaging charges	★ ★ ★ ★ ⯪

Feedback Time Chart

Feedback ratings are also presented on a time chart. If there is any negative feedback you can see how recent it is. If multiple negative feedback appears in the past month it is possible that the trader has lost focus and should be avoided.

	1 month	6 months	12 months
⊕ Positive	2	9	18
◎ Neutral	0	0	0
⊖ Negative	0	1	1

How to Leave Feedback

You will find the feedback link in My eBay with the details of the transaction. The link shown appears on the right hand side of the page. Click on this link to access the feedback form.

Feedback Form

You should complete the form as shown above. When you write the statement you should attempt to say something factual and meaningful to help other traders. Did the item arrive promptly? Was it well wrapped? Did the seller respond quickly to messages. These are the kinds of comments that work best.

Rate this transaction. This Feedback helps other buyers and sellers. ⓘ

◉ Positive   ○ Neutral   ○ Negative   ○ I will leave Feedback later

ⓘ The seller offered free P&P for this listing.

Please explain: [   ]

Detailed Seller Rating

The final section is for buyers only and concerns the detailed rating on different aspects of the service provided by the seller. It can be done quickly and should take no more than seconds.

★★★★★   Very accurate
★★★★★   Very satisfied
★★★★☆   Quickly
★★★★☆   Reasonable

Why Bother Leaving Positive Feedback?

Feedback lies at the heart of the community. Your trading experiences will be overwhelmingly good ones and you should always conclude with you completing the feedback form. Would you walk out of a shop without a word? Think of it as saying thank-you to the shopkeeper.

Brian was delighted with the Troika lamp base. He enjoyed excellent service from the seller which was reflected in the glowing feedback.

Leaving Negative Feedback

Think long and hard before you leave negative feedback. Sellers hate it. In general, it is permanent and you should only leave it as a very last resort, when you are certain of your ground. You should try to resolve matters in other ways. Also bear in mind that when a seller makes a mistake but tries to make amends he/she should receive positive feedback. We all make mistakes. However, bad, uncaring traders deserve negative feedback to warn others about them.

Seller Feedback

Originally feedback was left by both buyer and the seller. There were concerns that buyers could not be honest about a bad experience for fear of feedback retaliation by the seller. So in recent years the system was changed and now sellers can only leave positive feedback, freeing buyers free from such worry. If a seller is not pleased with a buyer's conduct they can leave positive feedback but reveal their unease in the statement.

How to Secure Positive Feedback

As A Buyer

- Carefully check out your seller before you bid
- Take time to carefully read the description of the item
- Make no assumptions about the item
- Email the seller with a question if necessary
- If you seller is unhelpful, tardy or curt, go elsewhere
- Pay up straight away, do not delay
- Check the item the moment it arrives
- Communicate immediately about any shortcomings
- Be diplomatic, ask rather than demand
- If happy leave appropriate positive feedback.

As a Seller

- Describe the item carefully, point out damage and flaws
- Include as many pictures as is helpful
- Give dimensions
- If it is heavy or light, point this out in the description
- State approximate delivery time
- Offer a returns option
- Send item promptly
- Be attentive to your buyer throughout the trade
- Listen sympathetically to your buyer's concerns.

When Val inspected Peggy the Calf she noticed his ear had been restored. She emailed the seller and tactfully informed him. The seller was unaware of the repair, fell on his sword and offered a full refund. They agreed on a financial adjustment and both posted positive feedback.

PayPal

PayPal on eBay

Several years ago there was a problem over payment of goods bought overseas and some traders resorted to keeping a stash of foreign currency under the mattress! Fortunately this has been resolved by PayPal, eBay's preferred online payment facility which has made light of former pecuniary obstacles.

PayPal

Buyers are encouraged to open up a PayPal account for their eBay trading activities. Its use extends far beyond eBay as you can use it for payment of all bills.

Sellers are now required to offer PayPal as a payment option. This means that buyers can enjoy all the advantages of this payment method if they wish to.

eBay Buys PayPal

In 2002 eBay bought PayPal. As a result PayPal is completely integrated with eBay and eBay traders can access their PayPal accounts through the back door via My eBay.

You will find this link on the left-hand side of My eBay summary page. This link, second from last shown, takes you to PayPal where you will have to enter your password to reach your account.

Shortcuts

Buyer tools
Close my account
eBay fees
Seller central
Safety Centre
PayPal
Leave Feedback

Advantages of PayPal for Buyers

- PayPal is free to buyers.

- It is quick and convenient.

- The goods are likely to arrive sooner.

- It can be used for all financial transactions.

- PayPal offers buyer protection.

- Mobility issues and cost of transport do not figure.

Advantages of PayPal for Sellers

- The convenience of PayPal attracts buyers.

- PayPal links make it easy to administer.

- PayPal offers seller protection.

- PayPal facilitates global transactions

- The money arrives instantly.

eBay has created huge opportunities for global collectors enabling them to pay for items located in foreign countries. You can stump-up in minutes from the comfort of your home. It is entirely flexible and if there is no money in your PayPal account the purchase will be funded by your bank account or your credit card, as directed by you. You will be informed as your credit card nears expiry so that you can replace it.

Register for PayPal

There are three different kinds of account :
- Personal Account
- Premier Account
- Business Account

The most convenient and practical for non-professional traders is a Premier Account.

Requirements for a PayPal Account

To set up a PayPal account you require:
- Email address
- Phone number
- Credit card or debit card
- Bank account details

(You need to link your card to a bank account and add a credit card to make full use of PayPal.)

Overview of Setting Up a PayPal Account

- Select the link to initiate PayPal Registration
- Complete the form
- Think of a password
- Receive PayPal email
- Enter your password
- Add credit card and bank details

Unverified Accounts

All PayPal accounts are initially unverified and have limits on sending, receiving and withdrawing money. The pre-verification limits are particular to each trader and depend on your credit status.

Corinne paid for this lovely necklace with PayPal. It arrived the very next day!

Verify Your Account

Account verification is an extra step that confirms that you are who you say your are. It is important to do this:
• To give other traders complete confidence in you
• To remove financial limitations on your trading
• To offer full PayPal benefits

How to Verify Your PayPal Account

• Go to PayPal account in www.paypal.co.uk
• Click the 'Unverified' link on the Account Overview page
• You will be guided through the process for verification.

Verification Process Involves

• Confirm your identity
• Comply with EU law
• Enhance your trading status

Account holder since 2002
Account type: Premier
Status: Verified (65)

Set up Bank Funding

Add your UK bank account to your PayPal account. PayPal deposit two small amounts into your bank account, which you will find on your bank statement. Log into your PayPal account and enter the amounts to confirm the bank account is yours.

Additional Business Information

Premier and Business accounts holders are required to fill in an online form to provide additional information about the items they sell using PayPal. If you are not a business you can select 'individual' and complete the form as directed.

Confirm Your Address

By taking a telephone call or receiving a letter at the address where you receive your credit card or debit card statements, you are proving that you are the owner of the card. PayPal is required to confirm your identity to comply with EU regulations.

Is PayPal Secure?

The security of PayPal is the number one question for most new traders. Are you really going to give out such sensitive financial details? Probably it is the safest payment method available. PayPal itself benefits from encryption technology which offers the greatest possible protection to your financial details. It also means that you no longer have to dice with the danger of sending out cheques. (When you send a cheque you are giving a complete stranger the name of your bank, sort code, account number and a sample of your signature!)

PayPal Fees

Buy – to make a payment is free.

Sell – to receive funds costs 3.4% + 20p

(Slightly more for cross border payments)

- Total cost £2.64
- Seller received £2.35
- PayPal charged £0.29

- Total cost £163.00
- Seller received £157.26
- PayPal charged £5.74

- Total cost £12.50
- Seller received £11.87
- PayPal charged £0.63

How Does it Work?

You can pay for items you buy on eBay, as well as other retail websites. You can pay with money held in your PayPal account balance or other payment method such as the credit card, debit card or bank account linked to your PayPal account.

Paying with PayPal

If you want to pay for an item you have bought on eBay with your PayPal account you simply select this as the payment method.

Total: £3.79 GBP

○ PayPal account (login required)

Receiving Funds via PayPal

If you receive a payment through PayPal you will receive an email notification that the money has been credited to your PayPal account.

PayPal

Hello C E Hixon,

You received a payment of

Your PayPal Account

You can reach your PayPal account at www.paypal.co.uk

PayPal Home Page

The home page offers an overview of your account balance. You can hold funds in several different currencies or opt to change them to pounds sterling.

Currency	Total
GBP (Primary)	£234.78 GBP
USD	$1.61 USD

PayPal Links

It also gives links to access and use your PayPal account.

Send Money

You can send money to anyone with a PayPal account.

Request Money

This link allows you to invoice another PayPal account holder. The invoice arrives in their email box and, with access to the internet, can be paid from anywhere at any time.

Add Funds

Transfer money from your bank account to your PayPal account.

Withdraw

Move money from your PayPal account to your bank account.
It takes 3 -5 working days.

History

View the details of your transactions for up to 4 months. Examples shown on next page.

Profile

The profile link allows you to amend your personal details, (email address, etc.) and financial arrangements. This is where you come to add or remove credit cards and make alterations to the financial set-up.

Profile

Add or Remove Email

Add or Remove Bank Accc

Add or Remove Card

Account History

You can check the activity on the current month or previous months in account history.

Monthly Account Statements	2009 May ▾
	2009 May
Reports let you track sales, disputes and mo[r]	2009 Apr.
	2009 Mar.

Understanding Your PayPal Account

The account page of your PayPal account itemises every transaction. In the example below there are two selling transactions and one buying transaction. The first is charged at 3.9% plus 20p because funds have been sent from Australia. The second is charged at 3.4% plus 20p because it was a UK transaction. PayPal is free for buyers and means that the Gross and Net sums in the bottom row are the same. The balance on your PayPal account is clearly marked.

Gross	Fee	Net Amount	Balance
£119.00 GBP	-£4.84 GBP	£114.16 GBP	£271.42 GBP
£163.00 GBP	-£5.74 GBP	£157.26 GBP	£157.26 GBP
-£2.74 GBP	£0.00 GBP	-£2.74 GBP	£0.00 GBP

Maggie does a little bit of buying and a little bit of selling and always uses her PayPal account. She pays her eBay fees from her PayPal account. She leaves the money she makes from selling items in her PayPal account to finance her little indulgences. In this way her eBay spending funds itself.

Getting Organised

Suggested Strategy for Success

eBay presents an opportunity that is particularly exciting for older people. But it is all too easy to jump in, make a mistake that knocks your confidence. It is best to start slowly and gradually build up your experience and expertise.

How to Proceed:

- For your first 10 transactions you should concern yourself solely with feedback. Feedback is the oil in the works of eBay. Ideally all your feedback should be positive but for your first transactions it is vital

- Buy from a Power Seller and study their auction page

- To achieve the best price only sell valuable items when you have a feedback score of at least 10 – 100% positive

- Start with buying. Buying is easier than selling and will introduce you to the process and a buyer's mentality

- Your first transactions should be unambitious ones, do not buy a car, a yacht or a garden shed

- Make your auctions sound friendly. Online transactions rely on exaggerated courtesy to spell out a desire to please

- Offer your buyers a returns option.

Getting Organised for the Long Term

Whether you use eBay occasionally or on a regular basis you should set yourself up for long-term trading. You need to:

As a Buyer

- Choose a User Name
- Choose a password
- Register as an eBay buyer
- Open up a PayPal Account.

In addition,

As a Seller

- Register as an eBay Seller
- Create an eBay Picture Folder
- Arrange your finances.

Who Can Register?

Anyone can browse on eBay but to buy and sell you need to be at least 18. It is comforting for everyone on the site to know that you have to register to buy and sell.

Choose your User Name

Your user name is the nickname by which you are known to other traders. You need to give it serious consideration as it is permanent. It needs to be something you can recall easily. However, it also needs to be unique and with millions of usernames already nabbed you might have to compromise on your first choice. The system will help you establish a user name and recommend alternatives if your first choice is taken.

> **User Name   pf3k8dtv82lnut5**
> I had a student who dreamed up a whacky and complicated user name. What seemed fun at first became increasingly tiresome as he had to look it up each time he came to log on. Make it practical!

Tallyhocollectables
Some sellers choose user names
that advertise their business and
special interest. It gives buyers
confidence.

Choosing a Password

Your password, on the other hand, needs to be something fairly obscure that is meaningful to you but that no one else can guess. Lots of people use family names and though this is tempting it is not very secure. Try a mix of numbers and letters. You should change your password on a regular basis.

Love Honour & eBay

Your marital vows demand you share your worldly goods but not your eBay password!

Register to Buy

- Name
- Address
- Telephone Number
- Email address
- User name
- Password

eBay contact their members via email and when you have completed the registration form you are asked to accept and agree eBay's User Agreement and Private Policy (read it carefully).

Once you have agreed to this you will be sent an email to confirm that your email address is correct. Open the email and click on 'Confirm Registration'.

You will be returned to eBay ready to start your search.

Register as a Seller

To sell an item on eBay you must register as a seller.
This is to verify that the seller is bona fide.
eBay keep your information safe and secure.

You need to have the following:

- A debit or credit card
- A statement that corresponds to the debit or credit card
- Bank account details.

> The debit or credit card is required for verification
> purposes only. You will choose how you want to pay
> your eBay fees later on in the registration process.

Seller Registration Form

Verify the information that eBay holds about you.
Provide credit or debit card information. Some of the boxes on
the form are marked 'if available', so if they are not applicable to
your card type do not worry about them. You need to provide
the address associated with the card. If you are using a credit
card you will need to provide your Card Verification Code
(Last 3 digits on reverse side).
Click continue.

Choose How to Pay Your eBay Fees

- You can pay your fees using the card just entered
- You can pay by direct debit using bank details provided
- You can pay using your PayPal account

Live Help

If you have a problem registering as a seller you can get help
by clicking on the 'Live Help' link to talk to a Customer Support
Representative during office hours.

Create eBay Picture Folders

Get organised from the outset and open up:

* eBay Selling folder
* eBay Sold folder.

eBay Selling

Upload pictures direct from your camera to eBay Selling. Look through the pictures and delete the sub-standard, only retain the best. Rest the cursor on the picture to check it is the right size. Name each file something that identifies the picture to you.

Necklace   Denim Skirt   Jacket   Jacket reversed

Toni Raymond Flour Jar   Corkscrew   Teabowl   Pine Cupboard

eBay Sold

When you have sold an item you can transfer it to eBay Sold, change the file name to the price achieved. Time flies and this will provide you with an archive of eBay prices.

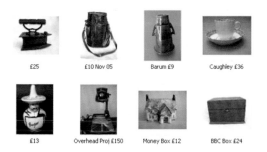

£25   £10 Nov 05   Barum £9   Caughley £36

£13   Overhead Proj £150   Money Box £12   BBC Box £24

Organising Finances

Most new traders like to open up a new bank account for their eBay activities. It means that you can keep your eBay finances entirely separate from your other incomings and outgoings and tell at a glance how much money you have made with your selling activities.

- Link your PayPal account to this account.
- Pay your eBay fees by direct debit from this account.

Then your eBay bank account is separate and easy to track.

Lizzie's Free Car!

Lizzie registered with eBay in 2005 and opened up a bank account for her eBay activities. She started off selling books and clothes but soon moved on to furniture. She turned her attention to the items in the loft that she had not touched for years. eBay fever overcame her and she found herself browsing in car boot sales for things to sell on eBay.

Her bank account built up gradually until she realised she had enough in her account to buy herself a second hand car. When her friends ask her about how she funded the car she says 'I swapped it for some junk!'

My eBay

Finding My eBay

Buy Sell My eBay Community Help

One of the most useful places on the site is My eBay. You should think of it as your home on the site as everything it contains concerns you and only you can go there. Your key to gain entry is your user name and password. You will probably go to My eBay every time you log onto the site and much of your activity will commence from the links you find there. My eBay plays a major role in keeping you safe from fraud. You will find the link to My eBay at the top of the home page. Click on it to go to your My eBay summary page.

Activity   Messages (2)   Account

My eBay is divided into three sections:

* Activity

* Messages

* Account

Click on the tab to take you to the appropriate section.

Summary of Activities

My eBay contains the summary of your activities. They are listed on the left-hand side of the summary page. The first is selling:

⛏ Sell

All Selling

Scheduled (1)

Active (2)

Sold (0)

Unsold (0)

Sell

In the example shown on the left-hand side there are two active or ongoing auctions. One is marked as scheduled, which means that the seller has created an auction but delayed the start. This auction will begin automatically at the allotted time.

Active

Click on the Active link to view your ongoing auctions. They are listed with a reminder of the main features of the auctions. To view the auction page you should click on the auction heading.

| Lowestoft 18th C. English Porc |
| Postage cost: £4.00 |

| Flapper 1930s Quality Pin Cus |
| Postage cost: £2.80 |

Watchers	Bids	Price
15	0	£170.00
9	3	£33.00

Active also shows how many people are watching your auctions (explained next page). It shows the number of bids and current price (those with bids in green). It states the time left.

Sold

Your item has sold! Use the Sold link in My eBay to progress the sale and send an invoice to your buyer.

Watch

Watch this item in My eBay

Watching is a way of keeping an eye on an item without placing a bid. It may be that you want to compare it with other items or prefer to place a bid towards the end of the auction. Perhaps you are a seller doing some research. You will find a link to place it in Watch this item at the top right-hand side of the auction page (underneath the item number). Click the link and follow the progress of the auction.

Buy

Beneath the summary of selling is the summary of all buying activity. In the example to the right four items are currently being watched. If you have placed a bid on an item you will find it in Active. In this example there is one active bid. Click on this link to see how the auction is progressing and to check on the current price and the number of bids. If you bid on an item but fail to win it, you can check on the final price in Didn't Win

Buy

All Buying

Watch (4)

Active (1)

Won (1)

Didn't Win (0)

Reminders

My eBay also offers reminders of your outstanding tasks. These are broken down into Buying Reminders and Selling Reminders. They offer convenient links to progress these tasks.

Buying Reminders

(Last 31 days)

☆ I need to leave feedback

 I can review 1 item that I

Organise

This section is extremely helpful for collectors and keen buyers. You can Save searches, for key words or categories, so that you are notified when such items are put up for sale. Click on the link to reveal a summary of the saved searches .

Organise

Lists (0)

Saved searches (10)

Saved sellers (3)

How to Save a Search

When you undertake a keyword search the number of results are shown at the top of the page before the list of auctions. To the right of this is a link to save the search. Click on the link to save the search and increase the number of saved searches.

129 results found for **red wedding hat** [Save this search]

How to Save a Seller

You will find the Add to Favourite Sellers link in the top right-hand section of the auction page in Meet the Seller.

Add to Favourite Sellers

Finding Big Ears

Carol, 57, collects Wade pieces and has built up a fine collection through eBay. She has saved a keyword search and is sent an email each time one is listed. She has also saved her top sellers. It keeps her in touch.

My Messages

A welcome innovation to eBay in recent years has been the introduction of My Messages. This is necessary because of the concerns about fake emails claiming to be from eBay. These are attempts by cheats to get hold of the IDs and passwords of honest traders for fraudulent purposes. As a safety measure legitimate communications are duplicated in My Messages. When you receive an email from eBay you should not respond to it without checking its authenticity. Go to My Messages to check that it is there. You can access the message by clicking on the title.

> **Re: cherrypiex has sent a question abou**
> **18:16:34 BST - MIDWINTER " ROSELLE "**
>
> **Re: cherrypiex has sent a question abou**
> **MIDWINTER FINE TABEWARE ROSELLE**

What you will find in My Messages

- Important alerts from eBay about your account
- Useful messages from eBay about buying and selling activities and events
- When you ask a seller a question or reply to a question you will find the communications in My Messages.

General eBay Announcements

- Security update – making winning bidder IDs anonymous
- eBay Shops upgrade: final reminder to check your Shop
- Retirement of old search system on 29th April for ebay.c

My Account

If eBay represents your house on the site, My Account is your study . This is the section that deals with all the administrative and financial aspects of your eBay trading. If you move house and change your address, or replace your credit card, you should click on the link to make appropriate amendments.

My Account
- Personal Information
- Addresses
- Notification Preferences
- Site Preferences
- Seller Dashboard
- Feedback
- PayPal Account
- Seller Account
- Donation Account

Notification Preferences

eBay like to keep closely in touch with their members. You will receive emails to confirm your activity every step of the way. However, eBay are aware that this does not suit everyone and you have an opportunity to tailor these notifications. Click on the link to access the notification options.

Feedback

One of the most important parts of the account section is the feedback link. By clicking onto this link you will have access to the feedback left by you and the comments made about you.

PayPal

PayPal is owned by eBay and much has been done to integrate the two sites. You can access your PayPal account by the back door by using this link. You will need your PayPal password to access your account.

Seller Account

This is where you check your accounts. eBay are meticulous about breaking down their charges and making them crystal clear to their users. You can check on the status of your account and change the way you pay the charges.

Finding Things

eBay's Vast Choice

With millions of items for sale at any one time eBay.co.uk presents a wonderful opportunity to shop for a bargain or something special but you need to know how to find things.

The Search Begins

There are two main methods of locating items which correspond to your regular shopping experience.

Let's assume you go to a department store to buy a thriller.

You have two choices:

- Find the book department and look for the thrillers
- Ask a sales assistant for the latest John Grisham.

This corresponds to eBay where you can:

- Browse the categories
- Keyword search

This brings up the list of sub categories.

> The unique Love Plaque (top), potted by Benny Sirota of Troika Pottery, sold for over £2,000.

Browsing the Categories

You will find the list of categories on the left-hand side of the home page. To start your search click on the category that interests you. This will take you to a list of sub-category links. The book category is conveniently arranged so that you can tailor your search precisely.

eBay Categories

Antiques
Art
Baby
Books, Comics & Magazines
Business, Office & Industrial
Cars, Parts & Vehicles
Clothes, Shoes, Accessories
Coins

Genre

Crime & Detective
Women's Fiction
Romance
Thrillers
More ▾

Narrowing it Down

At the end of the list (shown) is the More opportunity to bring up further options.

The thriller sub-category (below) contains over 28,000 thrillers but click on the tag to see Auctions only, Buy It Now or All items.

| All items | Auctions only | Buy It Now only |

28,665 results found for **Thrillers** [Save t

Honing the Search

You can focus your search by using the options on the left-hand side of the eBay page.   For example you can decide to look at the book auctions regarding particular authors. Just select the appropriate box. This brings up a shorter list of auctions for you to browse and consider.

▽ **Popular Authors**

☐ John Grisham (751)
☐ James Patterson (645)
☐ Dick Francis (463)
☐ Jack Higgins (444)
☐ Tom Clancy (398)
☐ Robert Ludlum (375)
   Choose more...

Keyword Search

Not everyone has the time or inclination to browse. For those who just want to buy-and-run you will use a keyword search.

thriller paperback john grisham|

Mysteries of the Keyword Search

The words that you put into the search engine correspond with the words in the auction title.

*   More equals less
*   Less equals more

If far too many auctions are revealed by the search you should type an additional relevant word into the search facility. If on the other hand there are too few, you can remove a word.

Alternately, you can extend your key word search to the title and auction.

collectable embroidery

☐ Include title and description

Search   Advanced Search

To conduct a more specific search you can click on the Advanced Search option.

thriller paperback   Books, Comics & Magazines ▼   Search

Combining Category and Keyword Search

You might prefer to combine a category and keyword search. By doing this you avoid totally unrelated items, that happen to have those words in the auction title, appearing in the results.

Refining Your Search

When you have undertaken a search you will be presented with a page showing a list of auctions. This is the shop window of potential auctions. Most will include a small thumbnail picture, called a gallery picture, which is designed to give you an idea of the item on offer and tempt you to take a look at the auction page.

A DARK DEVOTION Clare

THE SILENT AND THE DA

JACK HIGGINS - BAD CO

▼ Format

◻ Paperback (20,716)
◻ Hardback (5,873)
◻ Not Specified (2,082)
Choose more...

▼ Price

£ [   ] to £ [   ]

▼ Special Attributes

◻ 1st Edition (2,803)
◻ Signed (260)
◻ Not Specified (25,752)
Choose more...

▼ Condition

◻ New (5,122)
◻ Used (21,099)
◻ Not Specified (2,440)
Choose more...

On the far left hand side of the page are the options which enable you to save time by streamlining your search. In the case of the book search you have obvious choices such as paperback or hardback, new or used. However, you can also choose to see just first editions or signed copies.

Each category provides options that are relevant to the kinds of items on offer. In the clothing category you can select the size, colour, maker and designer.

In most categories you can select the level of cost that interests you and Buy It Now. You can choose to see only the sellers that allow you to pay via PayPal. You can opt to buy internationally or within the UK.

You can also:

- Research in completed listings.
- Find free postage and packing.

◻ **Completed listings**

◻ **Free P&P**

List of Auctions
Each search you undertake will conjure up a list of auctions.

Choose the Order
You can select how these are presented to you by making use of the Sort by option. These include:
Sort by:
* Time ending soonest
* Time newly listed
* Price, P & P, lowest first
* Price, P & P, highest first
* Distance, nearest first
* Condition, new first

Gallery Picture
Most auction summaries show a gallery picture that might tempt you to take a closer look.

Auction Summary Details
This provides the basic details of the auction including:
Auction Title
Auction format - Buy-It-Now or Best Offer
Number of bids
Current price
Cost of postage
Time left to run

This symbol reminds the buyer that the seller accepts PayPal as a payment method. Some sellers accept other methods indicated on the auction page.

Click on the Title to Access the Auction Page

MIDWINTER FASHION SHAPE "ZAMBESI" SMALL TEAPOT

Auction Page

You are now on the auction page. This is the very heart of eBay. Each auction page is divided into sections. At the top right-hand side is the item number, which identifies the auction.

> Item number: 180218600738

Meet the Seller

At the top right-hand side is the information about the seller, their feedback score and percentage. You can take the opportunity to read the comments that other traders have made about them. You can test the water by asking a question.

> See detailed feedback
> Ask seller a question
> Add to Favourite Sellers

Auction Information

At the top left-hand side is the information about the auction itself, including the current price, length of time left to run, number of bids, etc. There is also a blank bidding form in case you should be tempted to place a bid.

Auction Details

In order to discover more you should scroll down where you will find information about the item and auction, including:

- Description of item
- Report on condition
- Dimensions
- Cost of postage
- Shipping details
- Method of Payment
- Returns policy if offered
- One or more pictures of item (shown)

> The auction page is frozen in time but you can update it by clicking on the refresh link at the top.

Bidding and Paying

Before you Place a Bid

With so much on offer you are likely to see something that tempts you. With the excitement of the find you will be itching to place a bid but you should put that on hold whilst you do the following:

- You need to check seller's feedback
- Check on the terms of trading
- Look into the required payment methods
- What is the cost of shipping?

Investigate the Seller's Feedback

This is the most important check you can make. You need to make sure that the feedback score and percentage are acceptable. The higher the feedback and the closer to 100% the better. However, there are occasions when feedback is unfairly or mistakenly left by buyers and you can read the feedback comments. Fellow traders have the opportunity to reply to feedback comments left for them and sometimes the response is enough to put your mind at rest. When a professional seller receives negative feedback they do not respond with spite but in a measured tone relaying the facts.

⊕ Very promptly despatched. Would buy from again.

　Girl With A Pearl Earring (DVD 2004)-Scarlett Joha

⊕ excellent ebay very fast delivery strongly recomme

　LOST Series2-McFarlane Action Figure-JIN(SEALE

Terms of Trading

Sellers often write down the terms under which they are willing to trade. 'Payment within 7 days of auction end please'.

Returns Policy

In recent years sellers have been encouraged to give buyers a limited time in which to return the item if it falls short of expectations. Many sellers believe this pays dividends in terms of increased bids. The overall take-up on this option is very small indeed. You must find out who pays return postage cost.

Trading with Novices

It might seem harsh but some sellers are wary of new traders. Some request that potential buyers with a feedback score of less than 10, email them before placing a bid. This is a precautionary measure to ensure that the buyer is reliable and will pay up if they win the item.

Ask Seller a Question

If you have any queries or doubts about the item or terms of the trade you should take the opportunity to put them to the seller. Very often you will get a helpful speedy response that answers your question and puts your mind at rest.

On the other hand if the seller is slow to respond, unhelpful or unfriendly you should think carefully about whether or not it is wise to trade with them.

- See detailed feedback
- Ask seller a question
- Add to Favourite Sellers
- **View seller's other items**

Select the Ask seller a question link to bring up the form in which you type your questions. The seller receives an email and the communication is duplicated in My Messages.

```
Enter your question here
```

Cost of Shipping

In most cases the buyer pays the cost of shipping which is usually made clear to buyers. Details of the cost of postage can be found at the top of the auction page.

£3.00
Royal Mail 1st Class Standard Service to <u>United Kingdom</u> <u>(more services)</u>

Most sellers attempt to keep this cost as reasonable as possible whilst offering a speedy service.

For some bulky items, like this piano, the seller requires that the buyer picks it up. Buyer and seller would need to liaise over the arrangements.

Payment Method

eBay require that all sellers offer PayPal as a payment method. If you do not have a PayPal account you need to ensure that there is an alternative method that is accepted by the seller.

There are three different ways in which a buyer can pay for this piano. But some sellers will only accept PayPal and it is up to the buyer to check. Information regarding methods of payment is found at the bottom of the auction page.

PayPal	Accepted
Personal cheque	Accepted
Credit card	Accepted

Increments

eBay auctions employ an automatic system of bid increments. At low price levels the increments are narrow but as the price rises they become wider, rather like a conventional auction. Between £1 and £5 the increment is £0.20 but from £60 to £150 the increment is £5.

Proxy Bidding

This is a process for buyers whereby you leave the highest sum that you are prepared to pay for an item and leave eBay to bid on your behalf. It is automated and saves you watching the auction. You are informed by email if you win or are outbid.

The magic of a proxy bid is that you only pay what is necessary to win the item, up to your maximum bid. You may well win the item for less than your maximum.

How Proxy Bidding Works

Jenny has seen a pair of shoes but she does not want to pay more than £18. The current bid is £7 and she is required to put in at least £7.50 to place a valid bid. However, on placing this bid the message comes back that she has been outbid

 You've just been outbid. Do you want to bid again?

- Another bidder placed a higher maximum bid or placed the same
- Increase your maximum bid to have a chance to win this item.

The current price is £8. This is because the high bidder had placed a proxy bid. Jenny decides to put in a her own proxy bid of £18. She immediately becomes the high bidder at £9.50 (which means the other previous proxy bid was for £9) .With no other buyers tempted by the shoes and the rival bidder declining to place another bid, Jenny wins the shoes for £9.50 (plus post and packing as stated in auction details).

Placing a Bid

You want to buy this bottle of perfume
You have checked out the seller
You are aware of the cost of shipping
You have identified a payment method.

£14.99

(Enter £14.99 or more)

Locate top of auction page.
Type your bid in the form
Click the Place Bid link

This brings up a review page which reminds you of the basics of the sale. At this point you can pull out if you want to. Read it through and decide if you want to confirm your bid for this item.

Item you're bidding on:	
CHANEL No 5 EAU DE PARFUM 50ml NEW WITH OUT BOX	
Current bid:	£14.99
Your maximum bid:	**£14.99**
Postage and packaging:	£2.25 -- Royal Mail 1
Payment methods:	PayPal, Postal Orde

There are three possible outcomes after a bid

•   You are automatically outbid by a proxy bid

•   Your bid did not reach the reserve

•   You receive confirmation that you are the high bidder

You are signed in

✓ **You're the high bidder and currently in the lead.**
   • You may still get outbid, especially since your maximum bid

In the first two cases you can always put in a higher bid.

Bidding on Reserve Price Auctions

Some sellers put reserves on their auctions. This means that they set a reserve price somewhere about the start price below which they are not obliged to sell. The lowest reserve price that is allowed on eBay is £50.

£51.00

Reserve not met

Why do sellers use (and pay for) a reserve price when they could simply use the start price as the bottom line? The mindset tends to echo the sneaky idea behind setting a conventional auction reserve. They believe that the low start attracts wider interest and gets buyers interested in buying the item.

Sniping

This is the term for placing a bid in the final seconds of an auction and is widespread on eBay. Buyers believe that placing an early bid pushes up the final price. They hold out until the very end of the auction to keep the price as low as possible. It is important to understand that this holding-out mentality is prevalent on eBay as it is easy for new sellers to become despondent when their sales continue for days with no bids. It is possible that keen buyers are waiting to pounce, though this is not certain.

Should I Snipe for a Snip?

As a buyer wishing to pay the least possible for an item this is something you can consider, but novices should proceed with caution. I have received telephone calls from anxious students who have placed bids with the decimal point in the wrong place! With the luxury of time we were able to put this right but as last minute bids they might have spelled disaster. Only snipe when you have some experience under your belt.

 Congratulations cherrypiex, you're the

You Have Won the Item

When the auction comes to a close and you are the highest bidder, you will receive an email from eBay confirming the good news. There is a convention on eBay amongst conscientious traders that you pay for the item pronto and the seller sends it speedily.

Seller Sends an Invoice

Some sellers immediately send invoices to facilitate payment. This comes to your email box and offers links for you to pay. You should take this as a reminder and go to My eBay (below).

Pay from My eBay

Go to the buying section of My eBay and click on the Won link. It lists the auctions in which you have been successful. Beside the auction title is the payment link. This takes you to the payment page where it indicates the final price and the postage and insurance charge, when it applies.

▼ **Buy**

All Buying

Watch (5)

Active (3)

Won (5)

The options for payment are listed for you to select the one that suits you best. The system leads you through the process.

Pay now ▼

Send a Cheque

If you decide to pay by cheque you will discover the details on the auction page. You need to remind the trader which item you are paying for as some sellers are prolific. Get your skates on!

Payment by PayPal

If PayPal is the only payment method that applies this is the only option that appears. You have a chance to review and confirm payment. You will receive an email confirming payment.

Thank you for your payment

Checking the Item

When the item arrives you need to check it straight away and ensure that it is as described. Most items are exactly as the seller stated or better. In the event of the item falling short of your expectations you should get back to the seller.

Before you do this take a step back and consider if you are being reasonable. If so, you need to calmly explain the shortfalls. With diplomacy most problems can be solved. If you are pleased with the item you should say so in feedback.

Leave Feedback

It is most important that you take this last part of the transaction seriously. Sellers love receiving positive feedback, especially appreciative comments.

You will find the link to leave feedback in Won in My eBay. Click on this link to reveal the feedback form.

Leave ▼
feedback

Rate this transaction. This Feedback helps other buyers and s⊢

⊙ Positive   ○ Neutral   ○ Negative   ○ I will leave Feedba

Please explain: Thrilled with items. Speedy service. Thanks s

Keep your feedback factual so that it is informative as well as affirmative. The seller of this tin delayed sending it until the buyers were back from holiday. This flexible service was highlighted and praised in feedback.

Preparing to Sell

Preparation is the Key
Selling on eBay is easy when you get organised.

Auction Selling Form
There are decisions concerning each item and these are best done in advance of going online. You can type up a simple checklist of details that you need to create your eBay auction.

Packaging
Give some thought to packaging. It is vitally important that anything breakable is wrapped with extreme care. Most buyers find recycled packaging acceptable or possibly even preferable, providing it is supplied cost free. You may find it convenient to buy packaging materials on eBay.

Information on Postal Costs & Services
Discover postal and insurance costs at your local post office or online at www.royalmail.com. Kitchen and bathroom scales are very useful in working out postal charges. Royal Mail and Parcelforce are convenient and cost-effective carriers.

Get a Routine
You will be surprised how much time you save by adopting a routine. Make one day your picture day, when you take, upload and prepare your eBay selling pictures. The next day is for considering the auction details and researching items. Another day could be earmarked as your listing day. Some sellers allocate shipping days, which they publish in their auction details, so that buyers know when it will be posted.

Auction Preparation Form

Item
Dimensions
Category / sub-category
Title
Description
Start Price (Required)
Reserve Price (Optional)
Buy It Now Price (Optional)
Best Offer (Optional)
Duration
Start Time
Pictures
Gallery
Theme
Selling Enhancements
Counter
Payment Methods
Postage Costs
Post-to Locations

Useful to Have On Hand

Tape measure
Torch
Magnifying Glass
Weighing Scales

To Complete Sale

Packaging
Recorded Delivery Slips
Proof of Posting
Postal Service Receipt
Compliments Slip

When selling ceramics use a torch to detect minuscule
hairline cracks. Better you spot them than your buyer!

Researching in Completed Auctions

eBay auctions last for a number of days. When they come to an end you can no longer bid on them but for up to two weeks you can access them. Completed auctions are invaluable for researching your items. You can check to see:

Did the item sell?
What was the price achieved?

You can also study successful auctions and note:

The category
The title
The description
The pictures

How to Find Completed Listings

Having undertaken a search for an item you will find the completed listings option on the left-hand side of the page.

⊐ Completed listings
⊐ Free P&P
Choose more...

Caughley Porcelain – Completed Listings

11 Bids   £48.00   +£3.99
Sold

The completed listings search reveals a list of finished auctions with summaries of the results. For each it includes a thumbnail picture, the number of bids the item attracted, postage charge and final price. By clicking on the title you can access the auction page and read the auction details.

Choosing an Item to Sell

It is often said that you can sell anything on eBay but in reality there are some restrictions. You can sell most legal and moral items but you can check on the policy in Site Map

Dimensions

It is important to provide measurements of the item you are selling. You should point out if an item is particularly light or heavy.

Choosing a Category

This is a critical decision as many buyers browse the categories in search of something to buy. If your item is in the wrong category they will not see it!

For some items the category is obvious whilst others it is not so straightforward. In recognition of this eBay offer some help. At the beginning of the auction creating process you are required to enter keywords for the item which brings up a list of suggested categories. Select one of these or find an alternative.

Transported Back

The category for this Dinky Car Transporter is obvious. Buyers would expect to find it in:
Diecast & Vehicles, Dinky, Cars, Boxed

Getting Ahead

It is not so straightforward to allocate a category to this black ceramic head. Should it go into the Pottery category or would it best be placed with the hats? You would need to search completed auctions for similar items!

Listing in Two Categories

You have the option of listing your item in two categories. This can work well when there are two strong contenders for the category choice. You have to bear in mind that it will double your listing fee (though, if the item sells you will only pay one final value fee). Much depends on the potential selling price. If the item has a high value, putting it into two categories could substantially increase the final price.

Title

There is a formula to writing the perfect title.

- List all possible keywords
- Prioritise the keywords
- Use the first 55 characters as your title
- Arrange them to read as well as possible
- Put residual keywords in the item description

The title should include:

- Basic information. If you are selling a book in the book category you still need the word 'book' in the title.

- Model name, number and accessories are vital for modern hi-tech and electrical equipment.

- For clothes and shoes you should include the size, colour and material.

- Appropriate terminology aimed at your market. For example the US word for something with age is vintage.

The title should not include:

- Words like 'fabulous' and 'lovely' are a waste UNLESS you have characters left over. Think buyer's word search.

- Misleading associations such as 'not Kate Moss'

Describing Item
You need to state the basic facts about the item.

New Items
If it is the latest and most up to date model
Special features
Information on guarantee or warranty
Details or accessories and upgrades

Antique or Collectable Items
When and where it was made
Maker or designer
History surrounding the item.
Proof of provenance is a strong seller
Information about marks and backstamps
Point out potential uses

Example of Description

Fine quality early English glass

Hand made with ground-out pontil scar

Superb quality and fairly heavy glass

Elegant shape with the bowl cut at the base

Charming characteristics of an early glass

with some air bubbles and minute seed in foot

Ground out pontil scar in large foot

No chips, cracks or restoration

Approx 5 inches tall

Describing Condition

One of the most exacting aspects of creating your auction is describing condition. If your item is perfect and pristine you can state this. Anything less than perfection needs to be explained.

It is important to look things over very carefully. It is possible to own an item for years and not notice minor flaws. New does not mean perfect. Look at each item with fresh eyes to ensure that you are not making assumptions about it. The buyer is unable to examine the item so you must act as their eyes.

> You cannot afford to disappoint your buyer.

You must point out chips, cracks, flaws, tears, rubbing and wear and tear. If the damage is slight you should mention it and then dismiss it, for example:

- There is a minuscule hairline crack on the inside of the rim but it hardly shows.

Plan for describing condition
- Start off enthusiastically with the facts about the item
- Give details of damage and flaws
- Finish with a reminder of the appeal of the item

Useful expressions when describing conditions:
- In good condition for age
- A little tired
- Does not detract

Bunny in Bits

This Sylvac Rabbit looks fine in the picture but was smashed and glued back together. It is important that this is made clear to the buyers and possibly even pointed out in the title.

Start Price

This is the opening price below which bids do not register. Choosing the start price is one of the most critical decisions you will make.

Advantage of a Low Start Price:

- Low start price attracts more buyers
- Having placed a bid they anticipate owning the item
- Low start price results in lower listing fee

Disadvantage of Low Start Price:

- First bid may be the last, you are legally bound to sell

Buy It Now Price (BIN)

You can choose to add a BIN price to the auction. This means that buyers can bypass the auction process and opt to pay the quoted price for an instant purchase.

Advantage of BIN to Seller

- Adds urgency to an auction, bidders take action
- Sellers may receive the money sooner

Disadvantage of BIN to Seller

- Have to consider the correct BIN
- Sellers might miss out on the power of the global market

When a BIN secures a sale

Michael decided to go to the party as Tommy Cooper. The weeks flew by and all of a sudden he urgently needed a fez. Luckily he was spoilt for choice but the BIN on this one enabled him to buy and receive it in time for the fancy dress party. It arrived just like that!

Bottling Out

Jane considered a BIN of £45 for this bottle. It is onion shaped and very old (approximately1690) but chipped at the rim and badly scuffed all over its surface. But the damage did not daunt the collectors. The frantic bidding took the price to £138, triple the sum that Jane was expecting!

Reserve Price

It is possible to set a reserve price but not recommended. They are expensive and confusing and buyers hate them. The lowest reserve you can set it £50, so it is far better to use the start price as your reserve.

Duration

You can choose whether you want your auction to last 1, 3, 5, 7 or 10 days. There is no difference in the cost and it is just a matter of weighing up the pros and cons. The longer the auction the more people are potentially able to see it. But there is an idea amongst sellers that buyers lose motivation when they are faced with a long wait. In terms of the length of time 7 days is a reasonable compromise between exposure and enthusiasm.

Consider Your Market

However one of the most important considerations when you consider the timing of your auction is when it will end. You need your buyers to be available when your auction comes to a close. If your market is working people you need to ensure your auction comes to a close on a weekend or weekday evening. If your market is New York you need to do your homework and time your auction accordingly.

Buyer Anonymity

You have the option of letting bidders remain anonymous, which is welcomed by some buyers.

Start Time

You can choose to delay the start of your auction to a time that suits you. Scheduled auctions cost just 6p . This small sum is a wise investment as the timing of your auction (particularly when it ends) can be critical to the price achieved.

Pictures

The most cost-effective selling tool available. Covered in detail in Chapter 11.

Gallery Option

This is an extremely cost-effective auction feature that tempts the buyers

MENS WHITE DUNLOP GREEN FLASI

Theme

Liven-up your auction page with some graphic bling! You are bound to find one that suits you or your item, as there are many to choose from. Fun and affordable.

Counter
The free counter is useful to gauge interest.

Payment Options
Sellers are now obliged to offer PayPal as a payment option. You need to decide if you want to offer alternatives. Anyone with limited mobility or who lives a long way from a bank should consider only offering PayPal.

Postage Costs
It is important to discover these before you create your auction as buyers like to know the total cost before they bid. Buyers hate to feel they are paying over the odds. If you charge actual postage cost and nothing more you should state this in your auction page as it is a selling point. Canny sellers research the postal charges of the competition and set theirs a little lower.

Other Selling Enhancements
There are other selling enhancements that raise the visibility of your auction. Consider the cost in relation to the item you are selling.

The Blue Title
For items with decorative appeal you should ensure that you state the colour in the title. This nineteenth century poison bottle is so historic and poignant that it will be sought after by collectors. But its fine colour makes it attractive to millions of people who want to endow their space with brilliant blue.

eBay Offers!

At regular intervals eBay advertise special offers. These vary greatly from free listing days to free selling enhancements such as the small gallery picture. You can aim your preparation to making the most of these and selling the items that suit the offers. Some of the offers are designed to make eBay more attractive to buyers, such as the encouragement to offer free postage on DVD's.

Subtotal:	**£2.00**
Postage & packaging:	**FREE**
Total:	**£2.00**

Friendly Note

Prepare a professional looking compliments slip to accompany your item. Thank your buyer for their custom and remind them of your returns policy, if you offer one. Buyers like the idea that your satisfaction with the trade is your main concern. You can politely request they leave feedback. Happy customers add good sellers to their favourites. Come again customers are a lucrative aspect of eBay trading.

Or Write a Personal Note

Dear Mal
Well done on winning this
wonderful badge. It
belonged to my mother who
was a long term supporter
of the RNLI. I hope you are
pleased with it but in the
event of any problems
please do not hesitate to get

Pictures

The Importance of Pictures

Buyers can resist everything except visual temptation! Pictures are a critical aspect of your auction as they have the power to turn browsers into buyers. They are an opportunity to show off your item and flaunt the special features.

Many buyers harbour fears about bidding for things they cannot handle and examine. Carefully chosen pictures can put their minds at rest about the true nature of those items in a way that words never could. Even if the item you are selling is bog standard and everyone knows what it looks like, you should include a clear view of it.

Never stint on pictures and make sure you exploit the opportunity to the full. There are several ideas that you should take on board to make the most of pictures.

Cost of Basic eBay Pictures
- First picture is free (or included in the listing fee)
- Additional pictures cost just 12p each
- You can include up to 6 pictures with each auction

Picture the Opportunity

- The first picture must show the item as a whole
- Different angles provide maximum information
- Particular aspects can be highlighted
- Show close-ups of special features
- Designer labels and maker's marks are a must
- Be open and honest– show damage and wear
- Pictures of instruction manuals can help the sale
- Always include pictures that support claims of provenance.

There are no words that can adequately convey the charm of this old radio. It requires at least one picture and preferably several .

Items do not have to be old to melt hearts. This collectable cottage is modern, mass produced and standard but still requires a picture to push that sale.

Pictures tap into the hearts and souls of browsers and turn them into buyers. You also have to bear in mind that some purchases are carried out by parents and grandparents for their loved ones.

Showing the Marks

Collectable ceramics of all ages sell well on eBay. It is important to highlight the presence of a maker's mark in the auction blurb.

But it is essential to include a picture of the mark. Even if the buyer trusts that the mark is present on the piece, seeing it is a strong persuader. There are other considerations.

The marks may convey information to experienced collectors that extends beyond the seller's own knowledge. The impressed 'A' on the left of this brass weight means it dates back to early 18th century in the reign of Queen Ann.

Flaunting the Fine Detail

The devil (and desirability) is in the detail! Use close-ups to woo and wow the wavering buyers. Sellers are likely to be competing with other motivated traders and so any additional draw is worth the effort. Buyers are largely visually driven.

Picture the Flaws

Sellers must describe their items and mention damage and wear and tear. The documented damage to this old spice tin would deter buyers. A clear picture conveys its disarming appeal that transcends its flaws.

This biscuit jar dates back to the 1960s and is much sought-after. Although the jar is in good condition the wooden lid has seen better days. Sellers must do everything they can not to disappoint their buyers.

A close-up of the lid showing the wear and tear and missing knob gives buyers the best opportunity to weigh it up for themselves. Such clarity speaks volumes about the integrity of the seller.

Size & Scale

A picture is an opportunity to show the size of the item. This can be done in different ways using a coin, ruler or everyday item. This is in addition to giving actual dimensions

Consider the Setting

It is not enough to include a picture you must ensure that it enhances the auction and promotes the seller. Only careless sellers let the world and his wife glimpse their grubby draining boards with dirty dishes!

Invest in some large sheets of artists card in different colours. In this way you can ensure that lifestyle issues do not detract from the item. You can select the correct shade of background to compliment and show off the item.

An alternative to a plain background is to provide one that is appropriate. This hand-made ceramic pot is displayed in the artist's studio and looks wonderful.

Turn Off the Flash

You need to turn off the automatic flash on your camera. The flash leaves a bright spot that spoils the picture as shown in the example. It will take just a few seconds to alter the setting to turn it off.

Love the Label

Clothes, handbags and shoes sell like hot-cakes.   Designer and known makes sell best because buyers understand exactly what they are getting.   Name the designer or maker and include a picture of the label.

Even labels of everyday retailers such as Marks & Spencer, John Lewis, Debenhams, Clarks, Comet and W.H. Smith are a plus point in an eBay auction.

Vintage clothes enthusiasts flock to eBay and many global traders favour eBay UK. Use pictures to show off the selling features such as lace trimmings, fine embroidery and pretty buttons. Pictures help overcome the problem of describing condition

Taking Perfect Pictures

• Set up a simple 'studio' area

• Ensure the camera setting is correct

• Do not use the flash facility

• Take many pictures with different angles

• Delete the non-starters and take more if required

• Upload the pictures into your eBay selling file

• Name each file appropriately for easy recognition.

Digital Images

It is fortunate that the rise of eBay coincided with the dawn of digital photography. Many older people already own a digital camera or, if not, are open to buying one. They are useful for holidays, ideal for eBay selling. There is a wide variety available – you will be spoiled for choice.

Your digital camera comes with the following:

• The software on a CD to load onto your computer

• A USB cable to link your camera to your computer

• An instruction manual

• A quick-start instruction manual

Marvellous Memory Cards

Digital cameras differ from conventional cameras in that they do not record images on film but on memory cards. They allow you to view the pictures immediately so if they do not hit-the-spot they can be instantly deleted and the picture taken again.

Another bonus for eBay sellers is that the pictures required need to be small. This means that you can store lots of pictures on each memory card and select the best for your auctions.

Quick Start Instructions

Most cameras come with quick-start instructions which provide the basics to get you started. When it comes to instruction manuals sometimes less is more!

The Right Size of Digital Image

One of the least understood (but most critical) facts concerning eBay pictures is the size. In terms of KB they must be small.

eBay pictures must be under 100KB in size

The simplest way of securing small pictures is to alter the setting on your camera. Once you are familiar with your digital camera it will only take seconds to change the setting. Bring up the menu and select the size and quality option. Most offer options ranging from very large to extremely small. You require the latter. When you have taken your pictures and uploaded them into your PC you can check to ensure they are sufficiently small.

How to check image size

- Access the file in which they are stored on your PC
- Rest the cursor on the picture
- This brings up information about the picture
- At the bottom of the list is the file size
- The pictures look identical but are very different in size
- Left-hand side picture is too big at 861KB
- Right-hand side picture is perfect at 43.5 KB.

12

Create Your Auction

New to Selling

I recommend that new traders start with buying. It is easier than selling and you need to experience the concerns of buyers. To ensure that things go well in these critical first transactions, (when you are building up your feedback score), your initial purchases should be within the UK. Start your selling with relatively modest items and keep the money-spinners for later when you are a trusted member of the eBay community. Make it clear to your buyer that their satisfaction is your primary concern.

Checklist for Selling

You have an item to sell

You have taken and stored digital pictures

Seal

You have given them an appropriate name

You have examined the item carefully and noted flaws

You have thought up a title containing all keywords

You have written an enthusiastic but accurate description

You have researched the category

You have considered price

You have determined postal costs.

Start the Process

Buy Sell My eBay Community Help

Click the Sell link at the top of the home page to bring up the selling form. You will need to enter your password.

You Have Two Choices

The auction creating process has been enhanced over the past few years and you can now choose between:

- Quick Sell
- Advanced Sell

⊙ Quick Sell (not suitable for vehicles)
  List your item quickly using the most popular opt

○ Advanced Sell (Sell Your Item Form)

Quick Sell

Requires a limited number of details enabling a very speedy completion of the auction creation form.

Advanced Sell

Allows sellers to give much more comprehensive information about the item but takes more time to complete.

Which One?

Most standard items are suitable for the Quick Sell format. Unusual or complicated items are probably best listed in Advanced Sell. You can switch to Advanced Sell at any stage.

Choose a Category

Whichever format you decide to use you need to initially enter the key words to discover the best category.

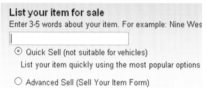

List your item for sale
Enter 3-5 words about your item. For example: Nine Wes

⊙ Quick Sell (not suitable for vehicles)
   List your item quickly using the most popular options

○ Advanced Sell (Sell Your Item Form)

Category Choices

Your keywords bring up a list of suggested categories. You can select one of these or opt to browse the categories for one of your own choice.

○ Vintage Clothing & Accessories > Women's > 1970s
○ Men's Jewellery > Pendants > Other Pendants
○ Women's Accessories > Other Women's Accessories
○ Women's Bags
○ Pet Supplies > Dogs > Clothing
○ Men's Shoes
○ Pet Supplies > Cats > Collars/ Tags

Okra Art Glass Vase

This individual vase would appeal to two distinct types of buyer: someone who wanted a decorative vase and Okra glass collectors. So, it was listed in two categories (Okra and Decorative items, Vases) to offer exposure to the different markets. Listing in two categories doubles the listing fee but, in the event of a sale, the vendor only pays one Final Value Fee.

Quick Sell

This requires minimal information for a speedy set-up:

- Title
- Category
- Pictures
- Describe Item
- Price
- Post and Packing
- How to receive payment
- Check fee for listing
- Save and Preview
- Check Fees
- List or edit
- Preview how the auction will look
- Preview how the auction appears in searches.

Click the link to list your item.

 Switch to form with more choices

Switch to Advanced Sell

You can switch to Advanced Sell during the auction creation process if you want to provide more structured detail.

Example of Quick Sell

Title

Think of the words that buyers would use to find it.

Large Hand Painted Earthenware Motto JugTorquayware

Category

The keywords bring up a list of suggested categories.

○ Pottery > Devon/ Torquay Ware > Dartmouth
○ Pottery > Devon/ Torquay Ware > Longpark
◉ Pottery > Devon/ Torquay Ware > Unmarked/ Unidenti
○ Pottery > Devon/ Torquay Ware > Watcombe
○ Royalty > Victoria (1837-1901)
Not one of these? Try browsing categories.

You can select one of these or browse for more.

 Dispatch Time - Please select a dispatch time.

You are nursed through the process and informed
when you make an error or omit something.

Adding Pictures

In my years of teaching eBay selling this is the part that concerns students the most. How do I add pictures to my auction? It is extremely easy! Adding pictures to your auction is similar to attaching pictures to an email.

Browse Link

The pictures section of the form contains the Add Pictures link. Click on this to bring up the Browse link. This accesses the files on your computer and enables you to locate your Pictures file containing your stored eBay pictures. Select your main picture first.

Your first picture becomes the thumbnail gallery picture so ensure that this gives the best overall view.

Click on Upload photos link

• To add more pictures repeat the process

• To remove pictures click on the Remove photos link.

Describe Your Item

Fabulous Mottoware Jug
Torquayware made in the West of England
Wonderful quality thickly potted
Probably dates back to early 20th Century or late 19th Century
Hand painted with fabulous stong vivid colours
Sensational mosaic pattern painted on upper jug
Saying etched into clay reads:

The man that drinketh good strong
beer goes to bed quite merry
and lives the life he ought to live
dies a hearty fellow

Just under 6 1/2 inches tall, 6 1/2 ins wide
9 inches wide at widest point
Excellent condition for age, no chips, cracks or restoration

Choose a Price

Enter the start price and the duration of your auction.

Start auction bidding at £ `28.00`   lasting for `7 Days ▾`

Postage and Packing

* You are prompted to offer different postal options

* Sellers are encouraged to be precise about postal costs.

How to be Paid

* Sellers must offer PayPal

* Sellers can offer alternatives

* Select the options that apply.

✓Accept payment with *F*

☐ Personal cheque

☐ Postal order

☐ Other (please provide det

Listing Fee

With the auction details selected you are informed of the listing fee. You will pay a fee (final value fee) when your item sells. In the event of it failing to sell, only the listing fee applies.

Fee to insert your listing: £0.62

Save and Preview:

You have an opportunity to assess:

* The completed auction page
* Your auction in the search results (below)

 Large Hand Painted Earthenware Motto JugToɪ

Place or Edit

You can return to the original sell form by selecting Edit Listing. You can change any aspect of the auction and review it again. Otherwise you can list your item by clicking the Place listing link.

Edit listing | Place listing |

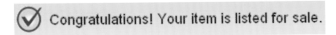 Congratulations! Your item is listed for sale.

Your eBay bidding, buying and selling activity is confirmed by email. When a scheduled auction begins you are sent an email from eBay to inform you.

Advanced Sell

There are many more options available to sellers.

The options presented vary depending on the item.

Examples of these:

Enter the item in 2 categories

- Online auction
- Fixed Price
- Buy It Now Price
- Reserve Price

Duration

Anonymity

Buyer Requirements

Returns Policy

Charity

Manufacturers name

Material

Date

Product type

New or used

Boxed or unboxed

Designer lister

Counter

The seller was not concerned about being interrupted whilst listing the antique chair as the system retains the most recent auction details.

Edit Your Auction

The first eBay member to see your auction should be you. It is important to check it to ensure that you are happy with details you have provided and the choices you have made. You can change an ongoing auction by using the edit link.

To Change a Live Auction

Locate the Revise your item link at the top of the auction page and you will be taken back to the sell form.

Revise your item

Sell a similar item

Create postage discounts

Add Pictures to a Live Auction

Click on the edit pictures link to locate the connection to your computer files. Use the browse link to find the extra picture.

Fee to revise your listing: £0.12 ?

Most changes do not incur a fee but additional standard pictures cost £0.12 each. You are kept informed of fees at every step of the way.

Watch Your Auction

Live Auction Action

Your 7 day auction (or number you have chosen) is under way! Can you relax and put your feet up for the week? Sadly, no! Having created an auction, you must keep an eye on it. You can make a dramatic difference to the outcome (whether or not your item sells and the level of the price achieved) by the actions that you take whilst it is live. You are going to be busy, busy, busy.

You must be prepared to:

• Assess the response to your auction

• Revise your auction

• React to information from the community

• Check your bidders

• Answer potential buyers questions

Check Your Emails

eBay keep you informed via email. They will send you an email when your auction starts and when it ends. They send you an email when a buyer sends you a question to help you respond to them quickly.

My eBay

You can watch the progress of your auction in My eBay. On the left-hand side of My eBay home page is the summary of your selling activities.

Active

Your live auctions are listed in Active. In the example on the right there are two current auctions. Select the link to see them.

Sell

All Selling

Scheduled (0)

Active (2)

Sold (1)

Unsold (0)

Active Summary

16	8	£78.28	2h 18m	Sell similar
4	0	£9.00	10h 11m	Sell similar

This summary gives brief critical details such as the number of watchers and bids (if any), the current price and time left.

To make the situation instantly clear, when your item receives a bid, the colour of the price changes from red to green.

Title Link to Live Auction Page.

Your live auctions are listed with the item title and postage costs.

If your item has received bids you can see the user ID of the high bidder.

Click on the auction title to be taken into the live auction page.

Flapper 1930s G
Postage cost: £2
High bidder: mrb

Georgian Antiqu
Postage cost: £2

Assess Your Live Auction

An eBay auction is not like a non-virtual auction where people bid throughout the process. Typically eBay buyers wait until the last minutes (or the nail-biting final seconds!) of an auction to place their bids. This makes it hard to assess the reaction to the item. However there are a couple of important indicators.

Watchers

When an eBay buyer is interested in an item, but not ready to place a bid, they place it in watch this item in My eBay. No one other than the watcher and the seller is aware of this. In the example on the previous page there are 16 watchers for the half-doll. This does not necessarily mean that they intend to bid (they might be doing research, or own something similar or they might just be nosey) but it is an indication of the interest.

Counter

Another good indicator is the visits counter. You have to bear in mind that this is not just a counter but a smart counter and only records unique visits. This means, if you and your 5 neighbours look at an item 10 times each the count only increases by six.

Visits: 00120   This Winstanley kitten has attracted much interest.

Counting on Kitty

With so many visits it seems likely (but not definite) that the kitten will sell. The one certainty is that members cannot bid without visiting your auction page. If your item only receives a few visits you should then question the title and category.

Revising a Live Auction

If you think that your auction is not attracting sufficient attention you can alter it whist it is ongoing. Changes are easy to make and can significantly affect the final outcome. There are many things you can do, including:

- Change the category
- Add a second category
- Change or add pictures
- Add promotional features, bold or highlight
- Add a gallery picture
- Add key words to the title
- Change the description
- Lower the start price

Restrictions to Revising Your Auction

Providing your auction has received no bids and does not end within 12 hours, you can:

- Revise anything in your listing except the selling format (it must remain an auction)

- If your item has received bids or ends within 12 hours there are restrictions to the alterations allowed. Go to:

Help, Selling, Managing Your Listing, Revising Your Listing to find the rules that concern changing live auctions.

How to Revise Your Auction

Locate the live auction page through the active sell link. Click on the title to reach   Revise your item
the live auction page.

Revise your item link takes you back to the original auction form where you can use the edit link to change any aspect you like.

Answer Questions

Whilst your auction is ongoing you are likely to receive questions from potential bidders. Welcome these enquiries as they are an opportunity to break the ice between you and your buyers. Make sure you answer these questions speedily and in a friendly manner. Never be curt or smart.

A Power Seller friend told me that most of the questions he receives are on matters that are clearly covered in the auction details. Instead of saying 'read it properly you nitwit!' he responds courteously. He is knee-high in regular buyers.

Where to Find Your Questions

eBay will send an email when you receive a question. Go to: My Messages in My eBay and use the link to answer.

Messages (4)

Bid History

You can discover who is bidding on your item via bid history. You will find this link towards the top of the auction page.

History: 8 bids

Check the Bidders

There may be occasions when bids are not welcome. You are within your rights to cancel bids on your auction if you are not satisfied about the track record of the trader.

- Their feedback score is not acceptable
- The feedback comments make you wary
- Your communications are negative.

Your Item Has Sold

If you haven't watched the exciting end of your auction you will receive an email from eBay telling you that your item has sold.

☒   eBay   You've sold your eBay ...

Go to the Sold link in the selling summary of My eBay.

Sold Link in My eBay

This reveals the list of successful auctions. Click on the title of the auction you wish to progress. This auction is no longer live but offers links to complete the transaction. You will find a link to send your buyer an invoice. Some buyers are quick off the mark and send the money via PayPal instantly, as in the example below. The money was in my PayPal account before I could exhale!

Sell

All Selling

Scheduled (0)

Active (1)

Sold (2)

Unsold (0)

Price	Sale Date					
£159.00	31/05/09	🛒	£			

The highlighted pound sign indicates that payment has been made.

You've sol

Dear cherrypiex,

Congratulations! ` receiving cleared this item.

Links to Progress the Sale

You will find all the links that you need at the top of the auction page.

You can view the details of the transaction to discover the address of the buyer.

There is a link to email the buyer.

There is a link to sell a similar item.

The Buyer Vanishes!

One of the most irksome things for a seller is when their buyer fails to pay up. eBay have responded to this problem by devising the second chance offer whereby the item is offered to one of the under bidders at the cost of their bid.

Additional Options:

▪ Send a non-winning bidder a <u>second chance offer</u>

(Sellers should not resort to this lightly but try to resolve things with the high bidder first.) Bear in mind that eBay will contact the winning bidder on your behalf. However, if the winning bidder fails to pay for the item the second chance offer is a good compromise. You will find this link in My eBay, Sold.

Your Item Failed to Sell

Not everything sells! However, if it is any comfort, the cost of failing to sell on eBay is probably the least cost of failing to sell there is! (The cost of selling is low and offers wonderful value when you consider the enormity of the global market).

Re-List Your Item

Go to the Unsold link in the My eBay to access your auction page. This offers links to re-list your item.

Beware Outside Offers

In the event of an item failing to sell you may be contacted immediately after the auction by an eBay member asking to buy the item privately. Do not sell off eBay regardless of how tempted you are. It is against eBay's rules and if things go wrong you are out in the cold without access to eBay's protection schemes. Re-list the item and invite them to bid.

Postal Insurance

Should I insure the item? Much depends on its value. For low cost items it might not be worth it as there is a small insurance factor in the cost of the regular service. For parcels travelling within the United Kingdom you might consider sending it Recorded Delivery as it is low cost and requires a signature.

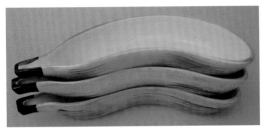

Toni Raymond 1970s banana split dishes £8 to £12 each

Forget the forms!

You might consider operating your own insurance for low cost items such as those above. Add a small sum to the cost of shipping each item. Make it clear that the cost of shipping includes postal insurance. If an item is lost in the post you can instantly return payment. The idea is that you will have built up a fund to cover the cost of a loss. It is a risk, but we are too old for all that form filling milarky!

Packing the Item

After all the preparation and activity you must ensure that you wrap the item with extreme care. There is no such thing as too much bubble wrap and no-one minds if it is re-cycled. Bear in mind most of the postal insurances cover loss not breakage.

Proof of Posting

Whatever you decide it is essential that you request a Certificate of Posting. In the event of a dispute it is vital.

Solving Problems

eBay to the Rescue

An enormous number of transactions are carried out on eBay each day and the overwhelming majority are successful. But occasionally things go wrong and steps need to be taken to get things back on track. eBay have experienced every conceivable problem and in response have devised a complete and comprehensive policy to guide traders through troubled waters.

If you have a problem or concern you can email Louise who will do her best to help you. She will need your user ID.

Help Link

eBay prefer that traders sort things out amicably between themselves but recognise that there are some situations that require their intervention. You should go to the Help link at the top of the page and browse the menu of options.

Solutions for Buyers and Sellers

You win an item but don't want to proceed

That's unfortunate but you are the legal owner and must pay for it. The best way forward is to continue wholeheartedly to ensure that you earn positive feedback. When it arrives you can sell it again. Enhance the auction and make a profit.

You have placed a bid for £100 instead of £10

There are only a few conditions under which you can retract a bid and this is one of them. You need to give the item number and select the reason for retracting the bid. Then you should bid again taking care to put the decimal point in the right place. Note that the seller will expect you to place a bid on this item.

Your item fails to arrive

Firstly you need to double check that the item has not been delivered. Is it in the garage or with your neighbour? You may discover that it has been returned to the postal depot. However, if you are sure, you need to contact your seller and give the details including the item number.

Your item arrives in bits!

It is very disappointing when an item arrives in pieces. The onus is on the seller to ensure that the item is properly packed. In this event the seller can request a picture of the pieces before offering a full refund. Standard postal insurance covers loss but not breakage .

The item falls short of your expectations

Be very careful. Were your expectations fuelled by your assumptions? If you are sure you are right, immediately get back to the seller and politely explain the shortfalls. He or she will offer a refund or suggest a financial adjustment. Much depends on the tone of your communication and in most cases it can be sorted out and positive feedback exchanged.

Item paid for but seller does not respond

You have tried and failed to communicate with the seller. You need to use the 'Won' link in My eBay to get help. eBay will contact the seller on your behalf.

You have found a blemish on your listed item!

You need to revise your live auction using the link at the top of the auction page. If you have received a bid you should contact the buyer. Explain the problem and offer to cancel their bid.

Your buyer has paid the wrong amount

You can return payment to the buyer for up to 60 days after the original payment was sent. PayPal returns the payment and fees so no-one loses out.

Your high and only bidder has pulled out

You need to request a rebate of the final value fee. Go to Request Final Value Fee Credit / Selling / Site Map.

You want no more dealings with a trader

You can prevent anyone you choose from bidding in your auctions. Go to Site Map / Selling Activities / Manage Bidders. Where you can add a member to your blocked bidder list.

Learn from their Experience

Aqua is not the new Green

Denise wanted an aqua coloured armchair and found exactly what she had in mind. Being cautious she investigated the seller and checked on the cost of shipping. But when it arrived she was shocked to discover that it was green. She checked the auction and realised that although it appeared aqua in the picture it was correctly described as leaf green!

You have to read the description carefully and take special note of colours as they sometimes appear different on screen.

Tight Squeeze in the Line-up

Gill lives to line dance and was thrilled to find these cowboy boots. She placed a proxy bid but won them at the opening price. The boots arrived promptly and she tore open the package with great anticipation. The boots were exactly as described: nearly new, dusky pink leather cowboy boots. However, they turned out to be boots for a seven year old child, hence the 7.
They were correctly listed in the children's category.

When undertaking a keyword search you need to check the category or start it off in the sub-category.

15

Safety and Security

Pro-active Safety and Security

The vast majority of eBay's millions of members are trustworthy and eager to promote and participate in honest trading. Unfortunately there are a small number of crooks that see eBay as a golden opportunity.

Their main chance is to trick unsuspecting traders into parting with money, or private details that enable them to further their shady dealings. However, in the same way that you can protect yourself from theft in your everyday life, it is possible to incorporate routine security measures into your online activities. The following will help keep you safe from fraud.

- PayPal

- My Messages

- eBay Toolbar

- Password

- Log Out

- Safety Centre

PayPal Security for Sellers

The best way of ensuring that you receive money safely is to use PayPal. There are many advantages, which are discussed in the PayPal chapter, but the outstanding benefit is that it keeps you safe. You do not have to give out sensitive details, such as your address, credit card number or bank account information.

In an effort to protect their members eBay have banned the use of Western Union, MoneyGram and other untrackable methods. If you are offered these systems for any reason at all (your buyer claims to have PayPal problems) you should refuse.

To accept an overseas cheque is a big risk as they take several weeks to bounce by which time your buyer is the proud owner of your gift! PayPal is a must for foreign transactions.

PayPal Security for Buyers

In paying for an item a buyer takes a leap of faith. The beauty of PayPal is that it is tracked and comes with its own insurance. A complaint from a buyer means that the money is removed from the seller's account until the problem is sorted out.

Paying with PayPal means that you do not have to send a cheque which contains your bank, bank account number, sort code and a sample of your signature!

Link your PayPal account to a bank account that is separate from your other finances.

Online security is not about luck!

Spoofs

Forewarned is forearmed! The chances are that when you become an eBay member, sooner or later, you will receive spoof emails. You should expect them. They are an attempt to trick you into giving out sensitive details but are of no concern if you ignore them or better still report them to eBay or PayPal.

Dear PayPal Customer,

We regret to inform you that access to your

eBay works with law enforcement agencies all over the world to track down the senders of spoof emails. They contain information that eBay can use to trace their authors. Forward them to:

spoof@ebay.co.uk

spoof@paypal.com

My Messages - Phishing

These are emails that appear to be from eBay or PayPal. They are an attempt to get your personal details to enable crooks to create fake listings to rob other buyers. Spoofs often claim that something is amiss and threaten to suspend the member unless they react immediately. Neither eBay or PayPal would request that you enter your details into the body of an email but would direct you to the site. It is easy to spot spoof emails. Go straight to My Messages in My eBay and see if the email is there.

My Messages – Pharming

Some spoof emails direct you to a fake website where it requests that you sign in with your user ID and password. These fake sites can look very convincing but the URL (web address) at the top of the page is not a genuine eBay URL. Go to My Messages in My eBay to see if the email is there.

Download the eBay Toolbar

This is a special feature designed to make accessing eBay quick and convenient. It keeps track of the items you have bid on and those you are watching. If you choose to enter your passwords, as is recommended, Toolbar's Account Guard feature can warn you when you are entering the same passwords into websites that are not eBay or PayPal.

Passwords

- Your password must be obscure, not easily guessed
- Do not share it with anyone as you lose control of it
- Use different passwords to eBay and PayPal
- Change them regularly.

Log Out

When you have completed your session you should log out.

Safety Centre

Security on eBay is constantly being enhanced and you can keep in touch with the changes through the Safety Centre.

eBay's Fees

eBay's Fees

Regarding the fees there is good news and bad news. The bad is that eBay charges are complicated but the good news is that eBay members are kept informed.

There have been several changes of policy regarding eBay fees and the best source is the site itself. You will find a link on the left-hand side of the My eBay summary page.

Shortcuts

Buyer tools

Close my account

eBay fees

Seller central

Safety Centre

PayPal

Leave Feedback

The Cost of Trading on eBay

Browsing and buying on eBay is free but sellers are charged a fee. This fee is composed of two parts:

* Listing Fee – this is non-refundable
* Final Value Fee – only applies if the item sells

Listing Fee

The listing fee is comprised of the insertion fee plus any extra selling enhancements you chose to take advantage of, such as additional pictures. The listing fee is charged regardless of whether or not the item sells and varies according the type of listing.

Understanding eBay Charges to Sellers

Listing Fee + Final Value Fee (if item sells) = eBay Fees
Insertion + Selling enhancements = Listing Fee
Final Value Fee is 10% of winning bid up to £40.
Car, Property & Media differ and should be checked on site.

Value Added Tax

All fees quoted include VAT at current rate for residents of the EU.

The Insertion Fee

This is based on the start price as follows. The prices quoted are for auction style listings of single items and do not include cars or real estate. There is a slightly different fee structure for Media products which include Books, DVDs, etc., check on site. Technology product charges also differ from the basic rate.

Opening Price	Insertion Fee
£0.01 – £0.99	No fee
£1.00 – £4.99	£0.15
£5.00 – £14.99	£0.25
£15.00 – £29.99	£0.50
£30.00 – £99.99	£1.00
£100.00 or more	£1.30

In a Reserve Price Listing, the Insertion Fee is based on the reserve price set by the seller, not the opening price.

In a Buy It Now Only auction the Insertion Fee is based on the Buy It Now price for your item.

Examples of Fees

Victorian Tile
Start price £2.59. Insertion fee £0.15
Sold for £4.50. Final Value Fee £0.45
Total eBay fees £0.60

Oak Blanket Box C 1750
Start price £50. Insertion fee £1.00
Sold for £335. Final Value Fee £34
Total eBay fees £35.00

When the Final Value Fee Applies

Final value is the last bid. The Final Value Fee does not apply if there were no bids or if the item fails to reach the reserve.

On Buy It Now auctions the final value is the Buy It Now price. There is no final value fee if the item fails to sell.

Final Value Fee

Not Sold – equals no final value fee

Sold – 10% of final bid to a maximum Final Value Fee of £40.00

Examples of Final Value Fees

The final value fee is clearly indicated on your account.

Fee Type	Amount*
Final Value Fee	£11.19
Final Value Fee	£0.90

Re-Listing Fees

If an item fails to sell the seller is encouraged to list it again with revisions that make it more attractive to buyers. This could mean lowering the start price or adding more pictures. Re-listing fees only apply if the item fails to sell. If the item sells when it has been re-listed using the links the seller is only charged one set of listing fees plus the final value fee.

This collectable football program sold second time around (for £50) so there was no second listing fee.

The Cost of Optional Auction Enhancements

Pictures
The first picture is free or included in the cost. All additional standard pictures cost 12p each.

Subtitle
A subtitle costs 35p.

Large China Beswick Flying Duck Mallard 1930s Damaç
Exciting restoration project

Bold
75p

Highlight
£2.50

Featured Plus – £14.95
Upgrade your listing to show up at the top of the same page it would normally show up in search results.

Featured First – £44.95
Showcase your listing at the top of search results.

Sorted Sells
Use enhancements to make your auctions appear professional. Show your item off to its best advantage. Describe your item fully and use the word processing tools to set it out neatly. State your auction policy. Sound efficient and accessible.

Reviewing Fees

In the process of creating your auction, but just before you submit it, you are presented with a breakdown of charges. It is an opportunity to consider your choices and make any amendments that you think appropriate.

Example of eBay Auction Listing Fees

Insertion Fee:	£0.15
Additional pictures:	£0.12
Gallery:	Free
Subtitle:	£0.35
Listing Designer:	£0.07
Total: *	**£0.69**

Checking Your Account

Activity   Messages (6)   Account

My Account

- Personal Information
- Addresses
- Notification Preferences
- Site Preferences
- Seller Dashboard
- Feedback
- PayPal Account
- Seller Account
- Donation Account

You can check your account at any time. Select the Account link in My eBay (you will need to enter your user ID and password). Click on the Seller Account link to discover the situation regarding charges. You can choose how you want to pay these charges and use this link to make changes to these arrangements.

Take a long term view of your selling activity and make good service your top consideration. Some items will make less money than anticipated but others will make much more.

Understanding Your eBay Sellers Account

Once inside your eBay seller account you can check on all fees. You can view your most recent or invoices up to 4 months ago.

Fee Type	Amount*	Balance
Final Value Fee	£11.19	£29.98
Final Value Fee	£0.90	£30.88
Gallery Fee	--	£30.88
Insertion Fee	£0.15	£31.03

Your invoice show the details of all your selling activity. eBay gives the running total of your charges.

Change Your Account Details

It is very easy to change your details. My eBay is a good start point for all such changes. Go to My Account in My Ebay. The Personal Information and Addresses links allow you to keep your details current. The Preferences options allows you to tailor the notifications you receive from eBay to suit your exact requirements.

My Account
- Personal Informatio
- Addresses
- Notification Preferei
- Site Preferences
- Seller Dashboard
- Feedback
- PayPal Account
- Seller Account

User ID and Passw

Account type

User ID

Password

Secret question

About Me page

Change Your Password

Use this link to change your password. The secret question allows you to identify yourself to eBay in the event of forgetting your password.

About Me page is your chance to tell members who you are and speak of your enthusiasm for the things that you are selling.

Terms Explained

About Me

Create a page that tells other members all about you. It promotes credibility and trust in specialised sellers.

Announcement Board

Where eBay tells the community about changes to the site.

Auction Buy It Now

An auction with a Buy It Now option. The Buy It Now option disappears when the first bid is placed.

Best Offer

This is an option for sellers of Buy It Now items that allows traders to negotiate the exact price. The seller can accept, decline or counter offer. Look for the Submit a Best Offer link.

Bid Cancellation

This is an action taken by a seller during a live auction. It is rare but happens when something is amiss. Possibly the item has been broken or the seller is not happy about the bidder.

Bid Increments

The steps by which the bids increase. They automatically widen as the price of the item rises.

Bid Retraction

This happens when a member withdraws their bid on an item. There are limited circumstances when this is allowed.

Browsing

Finding Items to buy by looking through the categories and sub-categories.

Buy It Now

An item can be listed as a Buy It Now or as an auction with a Buy It Now option to facilitate immediate purchase.

Completed Search

This is a search for an item that has been listed and the auction is finished. You cannot bid but sellers use it for their research.

eBay Pulse

A dynamic report on the fastest selling items on eBay. It is designed to help motivated buyers respond to the market.

eBay Stores

The success of the site had encouraged its broader evolution. By opening up a shop eBay sellers can capitalise on their success.

eBay Toolbar

A free download toolbar with potential security feature that offers easy access to eBay and helps keep track of items.

Escrow

A third party is paid a small fee to hold the buyer's money until they signify they are happy with the item. Used for costly items.

Final Value Fee

The part of the fee charged to the seller when an auction results in a sale.

Fixed Price

The Buy It Now price where there is no bidding and buyers can buy immediately.

Insertion Fee

The non-refundable fee charged for listing an item in an auction.

Keyword

A word put into the search engine to find a particular item.

Keyword Spamming

The practice of using irrelevant words in an auction listing to attract more attention.

My eBay

Your own personal space on the site where you find details of all your activities including buying and selling and sellers account.

My Messages

A security innovation to eliminate fraudulent spoof emails. Authentic messages are duplicated in My Messages.

Navigation Bar

The links at the top of a page that enable you to move around the site.

Negative Feedback

An unfavourable report left for a seller by a buyer that detracts from the seller's feedback score.

Neutral Feedback

A report by a buyer on a seller that is not positive or negative but which is considered to be a black mark.

Positive Feedback

A favourable report on a trader by a buyer or seller which adds a point to their feedback score.

Power Seller

Active seller who agrees to operate within particular high standards of trading and retain at least 98% positive feedback.

Private Auction

An auction where the User IDs of bidders are not displayed.

Proxy Bidding

Allows bidders to put in the highest sum they would pay for an item and leave the system to automatically bid for them.

Re-Listing

Using the links to re-list an item that did not sell first time round. The listing fee is waived if the second attempt is successful.

Reserve Price

A price that is higher than the start price but the lowest sum acceptable to the seller. The lowest reserve permissible is £50.

Scheduled Listing

Delaying the start of an auction to a time that suits the seller. This is usually to optimise the time the auction ends.

Second Chance Offer

In the event of the high bidder pulling out the item can be offered to a non-winning bidder.

Shill Bidding

This refers to the illegal placing of bids to artificially raise the price of an item.

Sniping

Placing a bid in the final minutes or seconds of the auction.

Start Price

The opening price for the item in an auction below which bids are not registered. It is determined by the seller.

Turbo Lister

An eBay selling tool that enables sellers to create multiple listings offline in advance of submitting them for auction.

Underbidder

The highest bidder beneath the winner who, in the event of the buyer not following through, might be offered the item.

Watch List

A buyer can place items that interest them into their Watch List which is accessed in My eBay.

Index